The Case for the Chief Data Officer

The Case for the Chief Data Officer
Recasting the C-Suite to Leverage Your Most Valuable Asset

Peter Aiken
Virginia Commonwealth University/Data Blueprint

Michael Gorman
Whitemarsh Information Systems Corporation

ELSEVIER

AMSTERDAM • BOSTON • HEIDELBERG • LONDON
NEW YORK • OXFORD • PARIS • SAN DIEGO
SAN FRANCISCO • SINGAPORE • SYDNEY • TOKYO
Morgan Kaufmann is an imprint of Elsevier

Morgan Kaufmann is an imprint of Elsevier
225 Wyman Street, Waltham, MA, 02451, USA

First published 2013

British Library Cataloguing in Publication Data
A catalogue record for this book is available from the British Library

Library of Congress Cataloging-in-Publication Data
A catalog record for this book is available from the Library of Congress

ISBN: 978-0-12-411463-0

For information on all MK publications
visit our website at www.mkp.com

This book has been manufactured using Print On Demand technology. Each copy is produced
to order and is limited to black ink. The online version of this book will show color figures
where appropriate.

Transferred to Digital Printing in 2013

DEDICATION

This book is dedicated to our colleague Burt Parker (1945–2010) who performed some of Data Management's foundational research.

CONTENTS

ACKNOWLEDGEMENTS

Major inspiration for this research came from in-depth discussions with Dr. Tom Redman and his influence is gratefully acknowledged.

The first author gratefully thanks the second author for our terrific discussions across the various issues. The exchanges were among the best in my professional career and I gratefully acknowledge the substantive revisions, enhancements, and extensions of my original remarks.

We acknowledge the effort of our reviewers who provided us excellent feedback on various stages of the draft — these included:

John Botega

Joe Cipolla

David Loshin

Lyn McDermid

Jim O'Brien

Anne Marie Smith, Ph.D.

Our wonderful acquisition/production team of Andrea Dierna and Heather Scherer contributed to the project at all stages.

Finally, both authors thank the literally hundreds of unnamed DM professionals and CIOs with whom we have worked, who have provided their insights, and who contributed to our understanding of this field as it is practiced and as it needs to be practiced.

ABOUT THE AUTHORS

Peter Aiken is widely acclaimed as one of the top ten data management authorities in the world. In addition to examining the data management practices of more than 500 organizations, he has spent multi-year immersions with organizations as diverse as the US DoD, Deutsche Bank, Nokia, Wells Fargo, and the Commonwealth of Virginia. As President of DAMA International (dama.org), his expertise in the practice is unquestioned. He has been a member of the Information Systems Department at Virginia Commonwealth University's School of Business since 1993 and jointly owns, with the University, Data Blueprint(.com) an award-winning, data management/IT consulting firm.

Michael Gorman has been involved in IT for over 45 years. He is the Secretary of the ANSI/INCITS Technical Committee on Database Languages, DM32.2 since 1978, co-authoring all SQL standards. Gorman worked for System Development Corporation which, with MITRE and Lincoln Labs invented data management. For the CIO of the US Army he helped develop their data management program including policies, procedures, and seminars. Gorman brought Database Management Systems into Federal Agencies including the Army, Navy, Air Force, EPA, HUD, Commerce as well as State and local governments. He also provided data management consulting to Fortune 100 companies. As CEO of Whitemarsh (www.wiscorp.com), Gorman provides consulting, methodologies, books, workshops and Whitemarsh Metabase, a metadata management system. He has authored numerous books, publishes regularly on The Data Administration Newsletter (www.tdan.com), and has taught at Universities, at DAMA Chapters, and International Conferences.

It's clear that technology is all around us, from your cell phone to your DVR. What we don't think about is the role that data plays. Technology is second nature to us and it's time for data to be the same. To truly tap the value of data we must manage it first, separately from technology.

My first exposure to the power of data was in 1989 and I found myself perplexed when people outside my organization didn't understand the concept of leveraging data to drive better business decisions and ultimately increase profits. At that time technology-based data implementations were a novelty. Data was limited in availability and its storage costs were astronomical.

Today everyone talks about data and information-based strategies. Technology's incorporation into all manners of business transactions is commonplace. Data is growing exponentially and storage is cheap. However, we continue to be challenged by the fact that the data isn't supporting the business to its fullest extent. Even in those places where the data is supporting the business, acts of heroism are often required to unite disparate data to unearth new business insights. It's difficult to quantify the challenge of disorganized data because strategies to create data architectures, independent from data's encapsulation within business information systems are almost non-existent.

Data materializes from within natural business transactions. It is inherently multi-dimensional. Because business information systems only capture parochially-based subsets of this data, much of its ability to be subsequently recast into different forms and uses is forever lost. Because of this business information system centric strategy, we continue to have suboptimal, single/restricted-use data that cannot be advantaged for the business.

If systems are built to support the business processes, shouldn't there also be systems that capture business data within its natural business-transaction contexts as well? If so, then Data Management's role is to enable the successful architecture, engineering, capture, storage, and ability to leverage business data to drive better decisions and ultimately increase profits.

While the journey to well-managed data and ultimately the use data to achieve a business's strategic advantage is long, it all starts with an organization's recognition of the independence of data from its encapsulation within business information system centric processes.

Data needs the same dedicated focus that technology has enjoyed if we truly want it to achieve its full potential. Now is the time to embrace the next generation in the data journey that must be focused on how to best manage that abundance of data and put it to work for the business.

The authors have dedicated their careers to educating themselves and others on best-in-class data management practices and through that work have a clear line of sight on how to ensure that the 21st century makes the most of this amazing asset. Peter Aiken and Michael Gorman have joined forces to describe the data challenges that most of us see but struggle to articulate, much less solve. I am hoping that all of you will see that these problems really exist and this book gives you the solution, which now in retrospect seems so simple. So, I challenge each of you, what will you do differently tomorrow with the information you will learn today?

Cathy Doss was Chief Data Officer of Capital One from January 2002 to December 2005. No one has challenged the claim that she was the first appointed CDO or that CapitalOne's CDO played a key role in its successful Information-based Business Strategy (IBS).

Cathryne Clay Doss

How to Obtain a Data Advantage

Data are an organization's sole, non-depletable, non-degrading, durable asset. This book makes the case for dedicating an individual to leverage them as assets — a Chief Data Officer or CDO. Only through a proficient individual:

1. Dedicated solely to data asset leveraging,
2. Unconstrained by an IT project mindset, and
3. Reporting directly to the business

can organizations expect to leverage their data assets. Data possesses properties worthy of additional investment. Many existing CDOs[1] are fatally crippled, lacking one or more of these necessary pillars. Often organizations have some or all components already in place but not operating in a coordinated manner. By the end of the book, you will understand these pillars, why each is necessary (but insufficient), and what do to about it. Briefly this book covers:

1. **Engineering our organizations to deal with the impending data tsunami.**
   Data and its use are becoming increasingly important to your organization. If you haven't already heard of **big** data and how it is 'transforming' your world, you will soon. Data's importance and scale continues to increase at an exponential rate. Difficult as it is to manage now, data management (DM) is going to get much more difficult, very quickly, based just on the forecast volume and dimensionality increases. In the face of this onslaught, we must transform our concept of DM and organizational processing: from part of IT, to supporting an organization engineered to leverage its data and surf the data tsunami.
2. **More than likely, you, your IT leadership, your organizational knowledge workers have not had opportunity to acquire the requisite**

---

[1] Our 2013 survey research indicated that 70% of current CDO positions had existed for less than one year, 19% had existed for 1−3 years, and 8% for 3−5 years.

knowledge, skills, and abilities (KSAs) to strategically leverage data as an asset.

Yet you are still responsible for well-managed data. You are all smart individuals who have proven capabilities, mastering technological change. You were never asked to learn about data and so didn't learn much about it. As a result, less than 10% possess the KSAs required to successfully leverage data assets [representing IP equal to half of organizational valuations (Olavsrud 2012)]. The other 90% are not data-knowledgeable.[2] Once the CDO/IT/non-IT knowledge workers are tasked, educated, and organized to leverage data, the organization's performance will propel it to the head of its peer group.

3. **(Until reading this) You may have been unaware that your IT leadership likely does not possess these KSAs.**

   You likely think of data as a part of IT. If you investigate, you will be disappointed at the time and type of attention that data gets. Fueling IT operations, data inputs and outputs must be exactly matched at the most atomic level in order to be useful. Your organization is probably spending much time, resources, and effort managing differing data requirements requiring inordinate transformation efforts. This constrains operations and saps resources − mainly from data analysis. Organizations made aware of these situations, rapidly reconfigure and take advantage of these new capabilities.

4. **Your IT leadership is similarly unaware.**

   Your IT leadership attended appropriate training/college and learned what they were taught. The subject of DM is often never introduced. Most encountered data only in a class devoted to database management system development. Having learned what they were asked to learn, IT leaders acquired a technology-centric view of data and are largely unaware of the need for architecture/engineering-based DM KSAs. Not being data-knowledgeable, they cannot be good decision-makers about data. When these circumstances improve, it is possible to calculate the ROI obtained from data leveraging and incorporate it as a strategic organizational capability.

---

[2]We did not use the term "data-literate" as this is a much lower standard.

5. **Your organization is likely unprepared to obtain a big data advantage.**

   Because of the above, your organization lacks repeatable processes for being able to successfully use data assets to support organizational strategy. Your data related activities are costing more, taking longer, and delivering less − your operations are similarly brittle. You are unaware of this and your organization is not taking steps to address it. Organizations making these changes are able to incorporate new technological capabilities into their overall architecture and obtain data advantages more quickly.

6. **Unless you *dedicate* an individual to leveraging data assets, your organization will continue be unable to obtain a data advantage.**

   To address this challenge, name someone to be your data Chief − most are calling it a Chief Data Officer (CDO). Provide them with the necessary success pillars.

   First, sole dedication to data. Fractional approaches have not worked to date − this is a full time effort. A committed focus to data-centric development (see Section 3.5) facilitates C-level data asset awareness.

   Second, de-linking data asset evolution from business information system development permits your architects to develop the necessary evolutionary, strategic mindset toward data.

   Third, this position must report up to the executive leadership. It is really a question of bandwidth. IT management cannot devote the requisite time/resources and is not data knowledgeable. Freeing the CDO from the IT reporting chain results in faster organizational transformation and permits increased agility.

'Working' from this perspective for at least a year, the CDO will understand your organizational data challenge − a prerequisite to data-knowledgeable decision-making (see our job description for the position included as Section 5.3.5).

CHAPTER *1*

Introduction — Speaking of Data (Big, Little, Dark ...) in Anticipation of the Impending Tsunami

As this book was being completed (2013, Q1), the Gartner Group estimated that 'big data' was 2−5 years away from peak hype. Their widely watched, reported, and adopted forecast indicated that buzz around the concept of "big data" would be increasing the near future. If you have not heard the hype − you will.

We are not going to bore you by re-creating a bunch of statistics showing that data creation, data processing, and data understanding requirements are increasing at increasing rates. Just consider the widely-cited fact that AT&T mobile traffic increased 8,000% between the years 2007−2010 or Eric Schmidt's often-repeated comment that, "Every 2 days we create as much information as we did up until 2003." It is sufficient to say that the number of things that produces data is rapidly growing. For example, 1 billion smart phones were in use in 2012. It should take only three more years to double to 2 billion (Brown 2012). Increasingly, individuals make use of the thing's (smart phone/tablet/sensor, etc.) data-producing capabilities. It all adds up to a number of challenges that are referred to as "big data."[1]

While it has so far proven impossible to define data as 'big,' it is possible to objectively categorize big data techniques, which are what have really been responsible for the so-called big data successes[2] (Figure 1.1).

---

[1]Truth be told, there cannot be any such thing as big data. First − all other data would then have to be labeled "small" or "medium." We are now left with the challenge of using vocabulary such as "dark" to refer to legacy data. Second, because no one has come up with an objective definition for "big data" − it is impossible to separate out any specific causes and effects to study. Any measurements, claims of success, quantifications, etc. attributable to big data must be viewed with appropriate skepticism.

[2]Appropriate processing trade-offs such as eliminating the von Neumann processing bottleneck, taking advantage of continuous availability; or eliminating human limitations − can be objectively evaluated along with other advances for potential organizational utility − as all proposed capabilities should be evaluated. If your organization suspects that it might be able to benefit from the application of big data techniques, or has already embarked on this journey, this material is a must read!

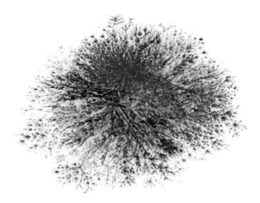

Figure 1.1 It is not possible to define big data (but there are a lot of depictions).

When considering data issues, a minority of decision-makers possess the required KSAs/background – they are not data-knowledgeable. Poor understanding of how to successfully leverage data prevents an organization from obtaining a data advantage by making poor decisions about data, its management, and how it is shared.

We have crystalized the reasons that have prevented most organizations from obtaining a data advantage. We advocate a CDO, responsible solely for organizational data assets. Through the CDO's perspective, the organization will understand what size and shape data challenge it is facing. Only then will the organization be able to make decisions about data using the appropriate context and understanding. We'll describe how the CDO should get started on this daunting task.

This book's contents can be visualized with the aid of Figure 1.2 – a word cloud of the text.[3] Sequentially, the next chapter describes the Chief Information Officer (CIO) function as having too broad a technology management to focus enough resources on data issues. The third chapter details 'exploiting a data advantage' and how the CDO function provides much-needed relief for broadly focused CIOs, who are ill-prepared to devote requisite time and attention. Chapter 4 presents measurements showing how organizations are not ready to leverage their data assets and what must be done to correct this. The fifth chapter examines the causes for this poor DM practice maturity and suggests remediation. It also argues that the remedy starts with a

---

[3]That the word cloud isn't on this book's cover is evidence of still significant technology understanding gaps in the industry.

Figure 1.2 Wordle(.net) of this text.

properly supported CDO as a business capability reporting outside of IT. Chapter 6 sums up and provides some implementation guidance. Organizations can soon be in a position to take advantage of the promise of big data techniques as well as more mundane DM benefits such as more effective/efficient operations.

CHAPTER 2

Understanding the Current C-level is not Data-Knowledgeable

2.1 CHAPTER OVERVIEW

We describe the reasons that C-level executives are not data-knowledgeable. To understand the challenge, it is important to understand leadership and symbolism requirements accruing to chief officer positions, as well as a needed technology management focus, and highlight the varied backgrounds brought to IT chiefs.

2.2 WHO IS YOUR DATA CHIEF?

If you picked up this book and thought to yourself:

Hmm — isn't the CIO the top data job?

Then you are exactly the person we are trying to reach. The short answer is:

Not in today's IT!

Before launching into what some have already viewed as a critique of the CIO function, it is important we state that CIOs have accomplished astounding feats, developed excellent organizational skill sets, and delivered tangible business value. In the process, we've learned a great deal about using technology to obtain a strategic advantage.[1] CIOs have our tremendous respect for the amazing results delivered by the organizations they oversee, the differing approaches to IT management, and reward systems (Wailgum 2009).

As a group, they have proven themselves astoundingly capable and quite adept at addressing organizational challenges – often by incorporating new technologies (clouds, analytics, service architectures, etc.) into complex environments. With rapid technology advancement, slow learners quickly fall behind and those who survive as successful CIOs have achieved extraordinary successes. But those who are successful are still largely not data-knowledgeable of the foundational role data plays in IT. Most organizations suffer from poor DM and a small but measureable number (less than 10%) think the approach we have outlined below is just common sense. An early reviewer of this book stated:

> I have worked with very senior, very talented CIOs. These folks fundamentally understand data – the complexity, multi-dimensional behavior and systemic flow of data. They understand the consequences of not delivering data to key operations. They understand the importance of data around operational risk and risk reporting. So it's not a knowledge issue – I believe it's a focus and attention issue.

We have to respectfully disagree with the reviewer.[2] Our combined 80+ year experiences[3] with more than 500 organizational DM practices indicate that 90(+) percent of CIOs are not data-knowledgeable. The data-knowledgeable 10% are inevitably surprised to learn they comprise such a small minority. As a group, CIOs have not managed to:

> Manage data as an organizational asset in an attempt to obtain a strategic data advantage!

---

[1]Unfortunately, from a learning/improvement perspective, it has been difficult to extrapolate lessons from their successes beyond case studies and surveys. Noted research (see Huff 2009 – two citations) has relied upon vagaries such as "the existence of a system" to assume capabilities, an unwise assumption given what we know of data quality (see also English 2009).
[2]Our guess would be that the nature of the reviewer's job attracted top-caliber colleagues.
[3]As of publication, 2013 Aiken has 30 years in the business, Gorman 50.

Data are an organization's sole non-depletable, non-degrading, durable, strategic asset. You can't use it up. If properly maintained, it cannot degrade over time or from use. It is by accounting definitions, durable – persisting beyond the one-year yardstick. Data's value increases as it evolves along the value chain. From business predications, it becomes transactions, and ultimately returns full cycle – the basis for future predications. So far we have failed to acknowledge data's primary potential value – factual information, fit for use, describing the organization's operations/environment and improving decision-making. When combined, these make data unique as assets in the organizational repertoire.

Data are assets that deserve to be managed as professionally and aggressively as other company assets. Objective measurements show that few organizations achieve DM success and are able to exploit a strategic data advantage (see Chapter 3, Section 3.4). In the face of the ongoing 'data explosion,' this leaves most organizations unprepared to leverage their data assets.

Returning to our title ...

If the CIO isn't the top organizational data job then what is?

The answer is that much of the care and feeding of data assets occurs at the technical level – if at all. CIOs/IT leaders and knowledge workers in general have little education/training in, and thus do not possess, the requisite KSAs to make decisions about organizational data. Being not data-knowledgeable, collectively, they don't know what they don't know. What knowledge they have has been acquired on the job and, because data can occupy only a fraction of their focus, not much OJT has taken place.[4]

2.3 CHIEF OFFICERS

The definition for chief is: "the head or leader of an organized body of people; the person highest in authority: the chief of police. dictionary.com

---

[4]Perhaps not surprisingly, knowledge workers tend to be more data knowledgeable – perhaps given that they work with it more consistently.

Organizations have recognized the need for individuals to be knowledgeable and accountable for important organizational assets and functions. Figure 2.1 is a (Wikipedia) list of 58 commonly used organizational titles beginning with the word 'chief.'

Chief Accounting Officer, Chief Administrative Officer, Chief Analytics Officer, Chief Audit Officer, Chief Brand Officer, Chief Business Officer, Chief Channel Officer, Chief Commercial Officer, Chief Communications Officer, Chief Compliance Officer, Chief Creative Officer, Chief Data Officer, Chief Executive Officer, Chief Financial Officer, Chief Human Resources Officer, **Chief Information Officer**, Chief Information Security Officer, Chief Innovation Officer, Chief Investment Officer, Chief Immigration Officer, Chief Geospatial Information Officer, Chief Knowledge Officer, Chief Leadership Officer, Chief Learning Officer, Chief Legal Officer, Chief Marketing Officer, Chief Marketing Information Officer, Chief Medical Officer, Chief Merchandising Officer, Chief Networking Officer, Chief Operating Officer, Chief Process Officer, Chief Procurement Officer, Chief Product Officer, Chief Research Information Officer, Chief Risk Officer, Chief Science Officer, Chief Stores Officer, Chief Strategy Officer, Chief Technology Officer, Chief Visionary Officer, Chief Web Officer

Figure 2.1 Fifty-eight commonly used chief officer titles (more exist).

The organizational expectation[5] is that the individual holding the title is the most knowledgeable executive in the organization and is responsible for the organizational asset referenced by their title. The Chief *Financial* Officer (CFO) is the individual possessing the KSAs to be both the final authority and decision-maker in organizational *financial* matters. The Chief *Risk* Officer (CRO) is the individual possessing the KSAs makes decisions and implements *risk* management. The Chief *Medical* Officer (CMO) is responsible for organizational *medical* matters. (The list continues ...) The organization, and the public, has similar expectations for any of chief officer.

2.4 THE BROAD TECHNOLOGY FOCUS OF MOST CIOs

The first uses for computing technology were to automate existing manual processing — making existing processes faster. As well articulated:

> *Fifty years ago, data management was simple. Data processing meant running millions of punched cards through banks of sorting, collating and tabulating machines, with the results being printed on paper or punched onto still more cards. And data management meant physically storing and hauling around all those punched cards (Hayes 2002).*

[5]For the finance domain, this is a mandate — the U Sarbanes–Oxley Act of 2002, enacted in the aftermath accounting scandals, requires at least one member of a public company's audit committee to have financial *expertise* (Congress 2002).

Tasks such as check signing, calculating, and machine control were implemented to provide support for departmental-based processing. Early on, there was no industry-wide approach to data processing systems development. The systems were the product of the creative minds and spirited individuals within departments (i.e. Personnel, Payroll, Inventory, Manufacturing, etc.). Each functional unit of the organization developed its own, siloed, data processing systems and data (see Figure 2.2).

These siloed systems worked well in isolation but requests for integrated data require significant additional development to accomplish the integration and large quantities of additional processing to achieve it. The description of the upward theoretical complexity required to integrate N siloed systems is:

$$(N * (N - 1))/2$$

Figure 2.3 graphs this function to illustrate the steep rate of increase in the quantity of integration-only based systems that need to be created. (In some environments, ETL comprise much of this class of systems.) To completely integrate the six systems shown in Figure 2.2, 15 different data interface systems need to be created to connect everything to everything using point-to-point interface solutions.[6] The red X on Figure 2.3 signifies the complexity point a large bank calculated as it managed 5,000 interfaces among 200 major function-based siloes. These numbers and complexity levels pervade all types of organizations and have held steady across decades — in spite of the advent of the ERP, SAAS, SOA, cloud, MDM or any other technology-based buzzword.

Each data interface becomes a data processing system in its own right (ETL, for example, comprises a major category of small systems). If you start with six silo-based systems, and add the 15 data interface systems, you end up with 22 systems required to provide point-to-point connections among six siloes.

As you can see from Figure 2.4 more than a few interfaces and the costs of point-to-point connectivity among siloes far outweigh their

---

[6]Six sources, if you count R&D as one big system. For that to occur the same integration must be accomplished within R&D. If not, then n rises to 8 — now requiring 28 interfaces for maximum connectivity!

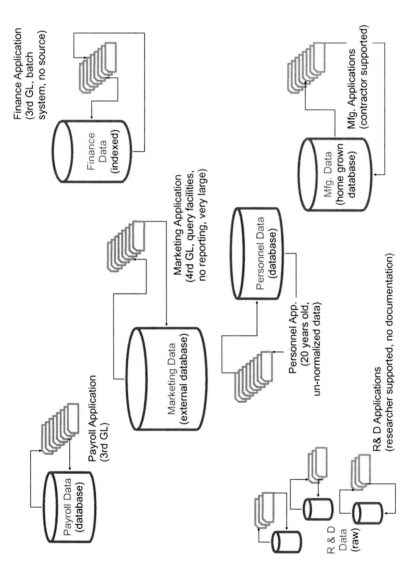

Figure 2.2 Typical organizational systems evolution resulted in application and data silos.

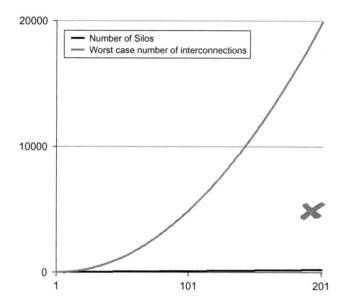

Figure 2.3 The rapidly increasing cost of complexity.

primary advantage – the solution implementation speed. When managing too much complexity, an organization's IT (and general) productivity decelerates. The more programmatically data interfaces can be managed, the lower IT's costs become.

Eventually, these arrangements required an individual-in-charge – a position that has evolved into the 'Chief Information Officer,' who is seen as responsible for all things technology. Wikipedia as defines a CIO as:

• The chief information officer (CIO), or information technology (IT) director, is a job title commonly given to the most senior executive in an organization responsible for the information technology and computer systems that support organization goals (Wikipedia 2012).

According to another definition, the CIO, is:

• The executive officer in charge of information processing in an organization. All systems design, development and datacenter operations fall under CIO jurisdiction (Encyclopedia 2013).

This makes both makes intuitive sense and also simultaneously accounts for much of the misconception. If CIOs manage the information

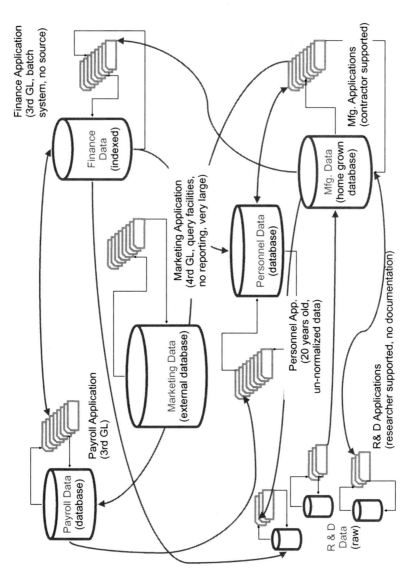

Figure 2.4 Typical organizational systems evolution.

technology, then is seems natural that they must also manage the information. Analysis (see Chapter 4, Section 4.4) shows this not to be true. Complicating further, is a lack of uniform CIO qualifications/preparation.

2.5 CIO PREPARATION – AGREEING ON UNIFORM QUALIFICATIONS

There is a general belief that the average CIO tenure is from 18 months to two years (Marks 2011). A search for 'CIO tenure' reveals a more diffuse picture. Recently, unsubstantiatable evidence has been introduced indicating that CIO tenure is approaching 4.5 years. In contrast, the information that the tenure of CFOs appears to have increased to almost 12 years in the year 2010 is easily obtained form the web (WEBCPA 2010). Some of this stability can be explained by a singular task focus.

CFOs have uniform prerequisite skills, certifications, and educational accomplishments. Professional organizations and recognized best practices uniformly dictate non-controversial KSAs. The Chief Financial Officer (CFO) commonly possesses a Certified Public Accountant (CPA), a Masters degree in Accounting, a Certified Management Accountant (CMA), an MBA, other recognized degrees/certifications, or at least a strong accounting background (Congress 2002). These are, widely recognized as necessary but insufficient prerequisites/qualifications and, applauded.

CIO backgrounds have much variety. A strong IT knowledge has been seen to be a big "plus" – with the other "plus" being organizational experience. While the lack of a "Qualifications Section" in Wikipedia is hardly proof, there is very little agreement on what is an appropriate background for a CIO. Popular CIO backgrounds include operations, finance, and sales/marketing (see Figure 2.5). Wikipedika continues, "recently CIOs' leadership capabilities, business acumen and strategic perspectives have taken precedence over technical skills. It is now quite common for CIOs to be appointed from the business side of the organization, especially if they have project management skills" (Wikipedia 2012).

CIOs come from a variety of backgrounds and are expected to master a wide variety of technologies as well as oversea a variety of technical functions. Despite a lack of formal, comprehensive, certifications

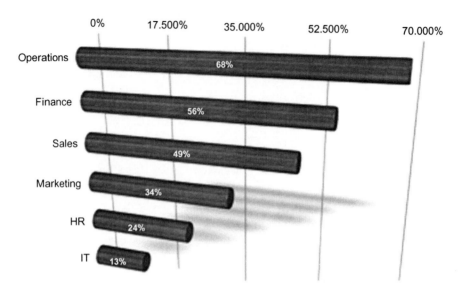

Figure 2.5 CIOs varying backgrounds (from McCafferty 2011).

and educational accomplishments, the CIO is the business executive upon whom is placed the requirement for the broadest skill set! These required skills include (from Curran 2009):

- Leadership abilities;
- Hands-on technology background;
- Experience in leading large change programs;
- Experience in running successful IT infrastructure operations;
- Management experience in a non-IT function;
- Innovative thinking that can solve relevant industry and business issues; and
- The ability to understand how projects and operations impact corporate financials.

Finding these in a single individual has been a challenge. A quote well describing the current situation comes from a former CIO colleague:

> *Advisors have been pontificating on the evolution of the CIO role towards CPO — Chief Process Officer. So now the CIO would own all technology, all processes and all data. No other organization is experiencing this evolution into other spheres of influence. The CHRO does HR work. The CFO does financial work. The COO does operations work. However, the CIO is expected to be the head of technology, the architect of all business processes and the intelligence behind leveraging data.*

Most CIOs today are challenged with being 'experts' on technology (infra-structure and application), business process, relationship management and data management).

None are successful at all and most have a bent towards only one of those areas, depending upon where they began their career and the path they took to attain their CIO role (Giuffrida 2011).

The management of data as an asset has almost never been seen as a significant CIO skill or job qualification requirement. Outside of previously referenced specialty programs, there are not many places that an aspiring IT executive would even encounter DM as topic of study. Smart, anxious-to-learn individuals, study, preparing for IT leadership – primarily through graduate curricula. They take classes and learn what we teach them.

A typical computer science/information/systems/ computer engineering degree includes just one course focusing on data. That course typically focuses on the *how* of building a database using Oracle, MS-Access/SQL Server, or an open source project.[7] A typical business graduate might be exposed to Microsoft's Access. Because DM is not a formal part of the curricula, they explicitly learn that DM is not part of what IT leaders do. As DM was not part of their education, it doesn't become part of their IT management purview. This technology focus provides the average IT worker with very little practical knowledge of how to best leverage data assets. As a result, very few IT or business professionals are data-knowledgeable.

In summary, while some C-level positions benefit from uniformly mandated knowledge, skills and abilities, the CIO function is lacking these consistent qualifications. Consistently, the CIO function has been not data-knowledgeable – there has been a lack of explicit, reliable and repeatable knowledge of how to leverage data assets. Because of the long-term planning required to obtain significant ROI, this results in IT leadership not considering various planning tradeoffs and making poor data decisions.

---

[7]Because a very small percentage of data management time is devoted to building new databases, one could make a very strong case for evolving the content of the "data course" to something more useful for future IT professionals.

2.6 WHAT ARE THE CIO DATA FUNCTION CHALLENGES AS CURRENTLY PRACTICED?

Because IT is complicated, organizations often find it more effective to concentrate technical skills in fewer specialists instead of teaching all knowledge workers to (for example) manage servers. IT attempts to create IT-leverage, using a few knowledgeable specialists that provide services to all. However, unlike most Chief Officers, who have real authority over their function area, e.g. CFO has real authority over finances, CIOs are generally:

- Not the ultimate authority on informational assets;
- Not able to devote the required time/attention to manage these assets;
- Not possessed of the requisite expertise to make good data decisions; and
- Not situated to achieve organizational data success from their technology/application-centric perspective.

Using the above criteria, few current CIOs qualify as data-knowledgeable.[8] Being not data-knowledgeable and using the title, these CIOs are *unintentionally* misleading their organization in two ways:

1. They are misleading them into thinking the CIO has focused requisite attention on leveraging the organization's data assets; and
2. That the CIO has the requisite KSAs and is capable of making good data decisions.

Our educational and professional support systems have left this 90% CIO group – not data-knowledgeable.[9] Section 4.4 in Chapter 4 shows that the CIO agenda is so overwhelmed that to divert resources to data management would literally force something else to be dropped – an impossibility for most. Only a fraction of these busy executives have reallocated options that don't hurt other responsibilities. This serious structural gap exists in most organizations and is a root-cause of many IT challenges.

2.7 CHAPTER SUMMARY

We presented the 'Chief Officer' function and the surrounding expectations, background, and preparations. We explained why today's CIO

---

[8]In many instances, addressing this challenge is as simple as reading the DM BoK!
[9]We did not use the term "data-literate" as this is a much lower standard.

is unlikely to be data-knowledgeable due to the lack of organizational DM visibility in educational/professional curricula. This has led to other problems impacting organizational IT success. We must remove the pressure on whoever serves as the technology Chief by creating a data Chief.

CHAPTER 3

Developing Your Organization's Data Leveraging Capabilities

3.1 CHAPTER OVERVIEW

One of the primary tasks facing our chief organizational officers is providing appropriate tangible support for strategy implementation. For example, CFOs engineer financial assets to ensure resources are available when required. Similarly, your CDO should focus 100% on leveraging data assets or:

Successfully leveraging data-based[1] assets in support of organizational strategy!

Currently, these capabilities are not easily available to 90% of organizations.

The data assets must be perceived holistically and more importantly, independently of technology, in the same manner a CFO "understands" the available range of financial assets and instruments.

---

[1]"Data-based" refers to assets that are essentially information-based in nature. It is used in explicit contrast with the term "database," which means *all* of the following: 1) the technology-based construct that contains data; 2) the Database Management System (DBMS) – software that stores, manages, updates, evolves, protects, and secures the database-contained data; and 3) the actual collection of data itself.

The concept "in support of organizational strategy" is foreign to those whose job it has become "to manage data." Most data professionals refer to *management* as being a goal.[2] Management is a necessary (but insufficient) prerequisite to successful data leveraging – leveraging is a higher order objective. Advantageous DM is a prerequisite to achieving organizational data leverage. Exploiting a data advantage is what brings recognized value to data assets. We examine seven related subtopics of exploiting a data advantage that are likely to be unfamiliar to your CIO/CDO.

- **Engineering Leverage**. Data is a mechanism for leveraging IT work products. Data enhances virtually all IT work products. (We like our colleague John Ladley's concept: data as fuel.) Thus, data fuels all organizational operations that employ IT.
- **Architecting Data Leverage**. Leveraging data is accomplished through architecture/engineering methods/techniques. We illustrate the difference in problem-solving approaches and describe data leverage goals.
- **Data Strategy Development**. To truly serve as an asset, data must support strategy. Well-engineered data strategies are supported by a goal, plans, projected work product outcomes, cost estimates, and ROI – along with an engineered plan to measure accomplishment. Data architecture reinforces data strategy.
- **An Alternative Approach to IT Development**. Data assets do not exist in isolation. They are influenced by data-centric or process-centric development approaches. Data-centric approaches are generally better and more difficult to implement than process-centric approaches. When created through data-centric approaches, data's leverage capabilities are extended.
- **Data Centric Principles**. Data leveraging needs to be guided by general design principles. These can be assessed for outcomes and contribution to goals.
- **Assessing Data Leveraging**. DM program execution needs to be regularly assessed. Without crisp mechanisms for measuring success, organizations lose focus on their mission.
- **Application Software/COTS Packages**. Data centric concepts apply specifically in largely package-based environments. They deliver specific concrete utility – several uses are described.

[2]It is an important goal – consider the question: *How can you secure it, if you can't manage it?* and the associated implications for the information security industry.

3.2 ENGINEERING LEVERAGE FOR YOUR DATA ADVANTAGE

Leverage is defined as: the mechanical advantage of a lever and as advantage gained by being in a position to use a lever. A **lever** then is defined as a rigid bar pivoted about a fulcrum, used to transfer a force to a load and usually to provide a mechanical advantage (dictionary.com 2012).

Figure 3.1 illustrates the leverage concept. Use of the term 'leverage' today means exploiting an advantage to gain a return on an asset such as staff, product, sales, or inventory. Equally important is that it derived from engineering, implying application and governance of engineering concepts,[3] bringing with it rigor and motivation lacking from the term "management." A critical leveraging characteristic is *investments producing increasing returns.* Points of diminishing returns can be calculated to guide decisions – ensuring that you don't invest more than you will get back out of something. (Note: data leverage also requires synchronized application of architectural principles – these are addressed in the next chapter)

Without the engineering discipline, it is impossible to effectively leverage data within the organization and with partners. Leverage is obtained using data-centric technologies, processes, and human skill sets. Leverage is increased as *r*edundant, *o*bsolete, or *t*rivial (ROT) data is eliminated from organizational data (Figure 3.2). Treating data more asset-like simultaneously 1) lowers IT costs and 2) increases knowledge worker productivity.

F, Fulcrum; *L*, Lever

Figure 3.1 Leverage advantage.

---

[3]Consider how inappropriate "financial engineering" due to lack of governance contributed to the 2008 fiscal catastrophe – see (Lewis 2011).

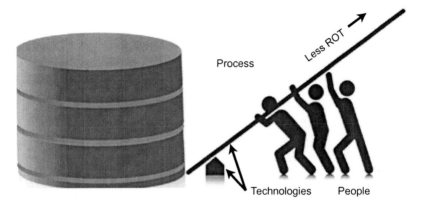

Figure 3.2 Leverage is an engineering concept.

Data's 'define once – use many times' nature permits it to be leveraged to great advantage. The natural consequence of this engineered leveraging is increased integration, interoperability, and non-redundancy. Leveraging through data architecture is an essential component that dramatically counters uncontrolled data growth and complexity.

Leveraging data requires specialized knowledge, dedicated resources, and sustained organizational commitment – components missing from data-unknowledgeable organizations. Quality results depend on leverage, and leverage requires an understanding of architecture/engineering concepts – missing from virtually all-education/training[4] and not part of most IT conversations.

Leverage enables hard numbers to be associated with organizational data – such as:

1. Degrees of ROT;
2. Amount of leverage; and
3. Data governance costs and benefits.

These numbers are required before it is possible to develop measurable strategic objectives. As with physical levers, DM has a tipping point. It pays off according to a step function, requiring a specific, critical effectiveness to achieve not just ROI but any results. Successfully investing $90,000 in DM will result in nothing if the required investment

[4]Some notable exceptions exist – DAMA International maintains an incomplete listing at http://www.dama.org/i4a/pages/index.cfm?pageid=3395

Figure 3.3 Engineering concepts applied.

was 100,000. As most IT projects exceed budget, failure in this area has caused organizations to shy away from these investments.

Engineering data leveraging affects the measures of success. It *improves quality* by reducing ambiguity and misunderstandings. It *improves productivity* by having the same collections of facts, concept structures, and database structures used over and over for as many purposes as possible. It *reduces cost* by eliminating the development of duplicate work products but whose sameness is obscured. It *reduces the risk* of reuse because the true nature, meaning and scope can be readily determined and thus their reuse can be trusted. One final data-leveraging characteristic − the bigger the data challenge, the more important data leveraging is to the organization based just on operational efficiencies.

Figure 3.3 illustrates application of engineering concepts. When determining the pictured machine's purpose, some helpful characteristics include the fact that it:

1. Is about six feet tall;
2. Has a clutch;
3. Was built in the 1940s; and
4. Is still in use today.

The machine is clearly a mixer but the sort of mixer engineered to cook for the thousands of sailors on the carrier USS Midway and for those who still enjoy the great ship's hospitality at events in the San Diego harbor. Clearly, a home grade mixer would been smaller and less expensive but could not have lasted through 65 years of continuous demanding service, much less provided the required instantaneous service levels.

3.3 ARCHITECTING DATA LEVERAGE

Architecture gives us the *innovative leveraging* component and the engineering gives us the *effectiveness/efficiencies* and the dimensions/considerations component. Architecture is also a discipline built on leverage. Consider how, office buildings are designed to include a certain number of male and female washrooms to accommodate the expected usage. How is the decision made to: provide one set of washrooms per office; one per floor; or one washroom facility for the building on the first floor? (Figure 3.4).

The easiest way to meet any instant demand would be to provide one washroom set per office. Although more convenient, it is not the best way to proceed. One set per office building *floor* is generally considered standard − providing the most flexible and adaptable means of satisfying current and future demand and it provides good leverage of the planned washroom facilities. Typically, architects do not overbuild infrastructure. Customers see it as both wasteful and potentially

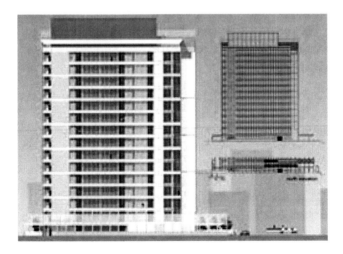

Figure 3.4 3D Graphics for Office Building Plan (from: http://www.michihito.com/14soft.html).

fraught with high future maintenance costs required to reconfigure to meet the demands of future tenants.

Similarly, decisions made about data should be informed with the same caliber of expertise and they simply cannot be as long as the outlined gaps remain. While almost all forms of IT work products are based on architectures, the focus here is on data architectures. These are what enable data engineering and leveraging. An organization's data architecture is the physical means used to achieve data leveraging. *All* data work is architectural, as opposed to software development that *can* be architectural. This has a dramatic benefit, improving: development; maintenance; understanding; and reuse for process/systems/software engineering components.

Figure 3.5 specifies relationships between the terms DATA, INFORMATION, and INTELLIGENCE. Intelligence is derived from understanding both information and it associated use. Information, in turn is derived from data and requests. Data is based on facts and meaning. Part of the elegance of Appleton's original model (extended here) is that it graphically depicts the importance of each architectural layer (depicted as building blocks) in organizational quests to leverage data. You cannot build a multi-story house on a marshmallow base. If the

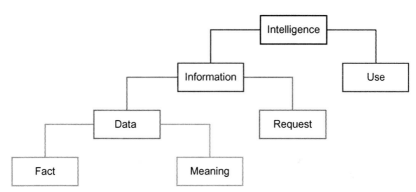

1. Each FACT combines with one or more MEANINGS.
2. Each specific FACT and MEANING combination is referred to as a DATUM.
3. An INFORMATION is one or more DATA that are returned in response to a specific REQUEST
4. INFORMATION REUSE is enabled when one FACT is combined with more than one MEANING.
5. INTELLIGENCE is INFORMATION associated with its USES.

Figure 3.5 A Model Specifying Relationships Among Closely Related Terms based on Appleton 1986.

foundation is unable to support the higher levels, the entire effort will be crippled. The intelligence layers must be developed using the specification and common understanding of the contained information layer. The dependency repeats as the data layer enables the information layer – both layers serving as foundational to upper layers.

Foreshadowing Figure 6.1 in Chapter 6, good DM practices must precede effective, innovative organizational data use. Failure to focus foundationally ensures that results obtained at the intelligence level take longer, cost more, and deliver less. Poor data architectural foundations explain the still-high failure rates of data warehousing and other specialist data initiatives – representing a particular threat to the allure of big data techniques.

The process of building the data architecture must be done inductively – based on factual information that already exists. This can be effectively and efficiently extracted based on techniques reverse engineering techniques that have been refined over decades (Aiken, Muntz et al. 1994). When combined with some exciting automated reverse engineering technologies[5] organizations can rapidly reclaim mastery over their data assets.

3.4 DATA STRATEGY DEVELOPMENT

Organizations maintain data-based assets in hopes of successfully employing them in support of strategy. In an attempt to provide valued products and/or services, a customer-relationship management (CRM) strategy might attempt to improve what is known about customer wants/needs. An organization may desire to transfer its inventory to its suppliers and to play only the role of transaction broker (Friedman 2005). A third strategy might be to use data to obtain significant efficiencies from productions/operations, ensuring a low cost advantage. "C" level positions are responsible for developing strategy. This sets direction, intensity, velocity, etc. as goal sets. Organizations maintain asset types to employ in support of goals. For example, receivables may be used as collateral for loans; real estate may be used to build literal store-fronts used to sell goods to customers, hiring many engineers and maintaining an engineering-supportive culture can build a literal brain trust of one or more types of expertise. In each

[5]See for example: http://globalids.com

instance, the asset is cultivated to further organizational strategic intentions.

As Figure 3.6 shows, basic confusion exists at the executive level concerning who is responsible for data strategy. The CDO is responsible for developing the organizational data strategy. Data asset-based strategies must be reliable, repeatable, and produce beneficial results that are clearly well beyond their costs. These range from tangibly, improved efficiencies to implementation of sustainable information-based strategies (Porter 1980).

For data, these can include tangibly improved operational efficiencies or sustainable data asset-based strategies. Studies indicate only 10% of organizations have board-approved data strategies (Eckerson 2011). Developing one jumps your organization ahead of the competition.

Developing a data strategy involves determining an organization's relative positioning on Figure 3.7, and developing a plan with measureable objectives to get better within their current quadrant and be prepared to move to the next quadrant. Organizational DM practices mature through a progression from Q1 to Q4.

For organizations in Q1, DM is not seen as strategically important to the organization and little is attempted in DM beyond "keeping the doors open." Data is not seen or managed as a strategic asset. Instead minimal efforts are expended as required to sustain operations (i.e., cash-balances instead of cash-forecasts).

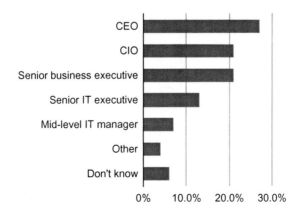

Figure 3.6 Who is responsible for data strategy? Source: Economist_Intelligence_Unit 2013.

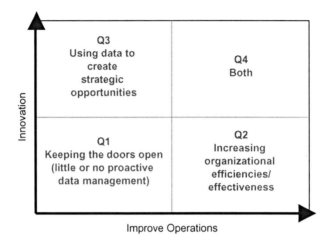

Figure 3.7 Organizational data strategy foci.

In Q2, organizational needs dictate a DM strategy focused on increasing organizational effectiveness and/or efficiencies. These might be applicable supporting a lean-supply chain management or low cost provider model. Importantly, Q2 is achievable without the need for additional investments in technology – a significant advantage.

Q3 organizations have achieved the ability to use data to invent or dramatically reimagine various business models. CapitalOne is repeatedly mentioned as one such organization – innovating around the idea of providing products for underserved credit populations (CapitalOne 2013).

Q4 organizations have become good at both Q2 & Q3 practices.

Organizations should typically progress through four stages corresponding to (both) crawl, walk, run and tangibly, improved efficiencies to implementation of sustainable strategies. Most organizations overestimate their data knowledge and attempt to accomplish Q4 data initiatives with only a Q1 foundation. The beneficial results are fleeting because the Q1 foundations result in a dramatic increase of data and business information system stovepipes that makes the IT infrastructure unsustainable.

Unlike Q1, Q2 requires development of specific internal KSAs. Q3 requires different and not necessarily complimentary KSAs. Most organizations overestimate their data knowledge and attempt to accomplish Q4 data initiatives using a Q1 foundation and neither set of KSAs. Given these circumstances, anything accomplished will: take longer; deliver less; and cost more than Q4 efforts built both on solid Q2 and Q3 foundations.

3.5 AN ALTERNATIVE APPROACH TO IT DEVELOPMENT

Most IT organizations do not incorporate data-centric development practices. These are required to produce the building blocks required for a data advantage.

Figure 3.8 illustrates the application-centric development approach. From the top:

- Determining the organizational strategy;
- Specifying specific goals and objectives required to achieve the strategy;
- Using goals and objectives to drive the development of specific combinations of systems and applications;
- Implementation of these lead to network/infrastructure requirements to support the systems and applications.

Data and information are identified, determined, and developed after other specifications have been articulated.

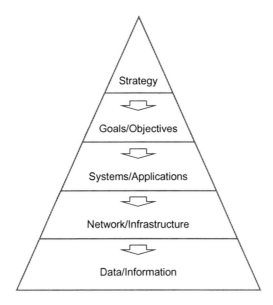

Figure 3.8 Application centric development.

Many organizations still find this approach worth doing as the ROI remains high. Challenges identified with this approach include:

- Processes and data are tightly formed around applications — making it difficult to maintain, and risky to change either.
- Very little data reuse is possible with an application-centric focus. Data names, semantics and use rules are encapsulated within applications. This makes their applicability across functions, departments, and the organization difficult to discern.
- Data specifications are developed exclusively from the application domain.
- Data requirements are driven from application requirements and are not based on the organizational requirements.

Figure 3.9[6] illustrates data-centric development. The first two steps remain unchanged but the third level is now data-focused:

- Determine the data required to measure goal attainment, base parts of the strategy on these data being employed widely, governed by a data architecture;
  These information requirements should be the only variable determining infrastructure requirements — all other network requirements would be associated with delivery platform implementation;
- Determine the network/infrastructure requirements to support the data collection, storage, updating, and retrieval for multiple functions across the organization;
- Identify, define, implement and deploy the specific systems/applications necessary to collect, store, process and report the data determined as needed to support the functions, organizations, and organization as articulated in the overall strategy.

Applications can be specified/delivered using smaller footprints focused on precisely articulated goals expressed by the data architecture. More importantly, through data and structure reuse, organizational system design is at least an order of magnitude less complex. Advantages of the data-centric approach include:

- Data assets are developed from integrated, organization-wide perspectives;

[6]We are indebted to Douglas Bagley (dougbagley73@gmail.com) for this conceptualization.

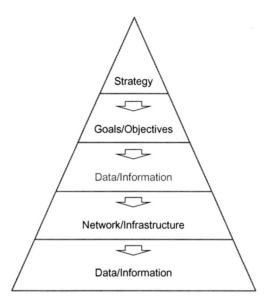

Figure 3.9 Data-centric development.

- Systems support organizational data needs and compliment organizational process flows;
- Elimination of application/system brittleness as data specification are separated, enabling it to be maintained independently;
- Data reuse is maximized — like a share buy-back this is pure mathematics it can only *help* organizations achieve agility;
- Enhanced data shareability and maintainability, particularly in cross-functional sharing;
- Significant reduction in the quality/complexity of applications/systems-wide perspective of their shared data — this leads to a reduction in systems creation; and
- Significant reduction in data interface quantities due to higher data reuse.

To be fair, there are some challenges identified with data-centric development:

- Perceiving and accommodating the application system needs for data (which may ultimately be unique to given applications) and to associate them effectively and efficiently within and across functions, organizations and/or organization-wide data requirements can be difficult; and

- Ensuring that as application needs evolve that the data architecture does not hinder the evolution;
- Engineering data structure generalization for maximum reuse.

3.6 DATA CENTRIC PRINCIPLES

Organizations can prepare for future change by adopting our principals as a starting place to guide their data strategy goals. They are:

1. Focus data assets to efficiently and effectively support organizational strategy.
2. Increase the available resources by lowering the resources spent on maintenance activities.
3. Reduce organizational data ROT.
4. Remaining data will receive more 'attention' with respect to quality/security/reuse.
5. Reduce the amount and complexity of the organizational code-base.
6. Reduce the amount of time and effort and risk associated with IT projects.
7. Engineer flexibility and adaptability into data architectures instead of attempting to retrofit changes after they are in production.
8. Produce more, reusable data-focused work products.
9. When faced with a choice between chaos versus understanding, organizations will gravitate towards a cheaper, more understandable solution.
10. Same comment as point 9 when comparing complexity versus ease of implementation.
11. Decrease the time spend understanding versus time spent focused on data-centric strategy.
12. Reduce uncertain benefits and increase engineering-based benefit calculations.

When followed, these support data-centric development, helping to prepare for future change by implementing a flexible, adaptable, broadly useful data architecture.

3.7 ASSESSING DATA LEVERAGING

Objective criteria need to be developed and used to assess whether your organization is objectively exploiting a data advantage. The assessment criterion consists of two parts: involvement and commitment. First there must be an organizational commitment to learn what it now doesn't know. Second, it must commit to an ongoing program — results here must be measured across years not quarters.[7] The first achievement is to demonstrate improving your ability to leverage data strategically.

An organization is objectively improving its data advantage if the organization is able to demonstrate that it has used objective data to improve its existing process. If it does this, then by definition, it must have an existing process that works.

This involves demonstrating: 1) that it is improving its people, processes, and technologies surrounding data management, and 2) it is using this knowledge to improve the effectiveness of "1"). Both are illustrated in Figure 3.10.

This sounds somewhat of a high standard but really just represents what should be best practices. If you have an important process incorporated into your organization, shouldn't you periodically evaluate its continued use and effectiveness? In order to perform this analysis you need to understand the process well enough to get meaningful data from it. How otherwise would any process improvements be evaluated objectively?

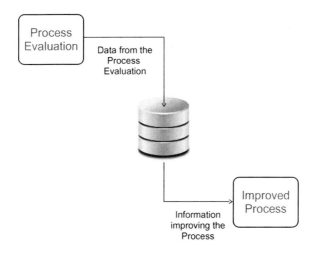

Figure 3.10 Leveraging data in support of strategy — *improvement process and criteria.*

[7]Thanks to Lewis Broome for his advice; *Don't dabble in data management!*

3.8 APPLICATION SOFTWARE/COTS PACKAGES

Many readers who get to this point may say, "What of the commercial off the shelf (COTS) software packages?

Doesn't our movement toward packages and ERP, etc. negate the effects of organizational data architecture?

If you are like most, your packages are driving your IT spend. Acquired under prior conditions (i.e. you inherited them), they are likely the focus of much IT management attention.

Your existing software application architecture is likely complex and was implemented in an application-centric manner. An immediate, useful role data architecture can play is a mapping function. Figure 3.11 illustrates this simplest, most-used form of mapping – the data architecture literally becomes the blueprint for the organizational integration activities.

If your organization benefits from an ERP, SAAS or otherwise con-solidated application solution you might be tempted to think that it plays the role of the data architecture. And it can – to the extent that your existing processes conform to the application's internal picture of its processes. Unfortunately these are typically unknown. When known, they can provide portions of the architecture, usually transac-tionally focused. Application-centric architectures rarely offer direct

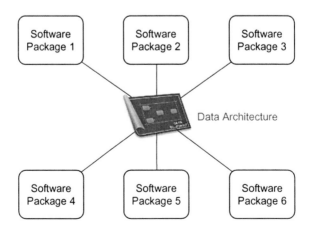

Figure 3.11 Your data architecture maps interactions between and across software packages.

data support of strategy. These components still need to be developed to understand your environment, holistically.

Data-centric practices can be most useful in these environments by guiding application package selection and evaluating proposed solution functionality. Ideally this should occur prior to any purchases but realistically must be implemented to impact subsequent implementations. Once you understand your existing data architecture, it is easy to identify processing gaps that can be filled by additional processing capabilities.

The first decision that data centrism can help you with is the build versus buy decision. The architecture will *specify* the data and provide information needed to *contextualize* and *constrain* the application requirements. Conventional wisdom dictates that packages are cheaper than evolving a legacy environment but now you will have information enabling you to make better informed build versus buy decisions. Armed with this information, many of our customers are choosing to build (at a lower cost) than acquiring packages. Either way the analysis has prevented over-investments in, mismatched software purchases.

When comparing among, and selecting from, potential applications, another data-centric practice requires offerors to present both physical and logical data models of their applications for comparison with the existing environment's requirements. Failure to comply results in offerings being dropped from the 'competition.' Fact-based, data analysis of package compatibility can provide organizations with out-of-the-box matches with your existing environment, often speeding up implementation. In cases of imperfect requirements matches, the transformation costs required to either change organizational practices or modify the software can now be incorporated into existing selection criteria. Finally, architectural impacts can be formally evaluated and instances requiring software/architecture modification can be better-documented using data centrism techniques.

Software packages capture, manipulate, report, and update data. Metadata recovered from legacy software also often describes internal processes. While the percentage of 'labels' within a module attributable to fact-names versus process-names is not easily known, there can be an immediate improvement in the software understanding when the data facts are immediately available, contextually, and across the entire software module if supported by appropriate metadata practices.

Data leverage benefits extend beyond architecture engineering. Enhanced, too, are all forms of human understanding such as user-help processes, user guides, technical manuals, and other System Development Life Cycle work product/specifications.

Failure to use data centrism in a packages environment means that organizations are unable to benefit from specific, measureable integration characteristics — forcing decisions to be made on little or no available information about their data. Data centrism allows packaged environments to be evolved at a lower total cost of ownership than today's application-centric environments.

3.9 CHAPTER SUMMARY

This chapter covered: What data is; how leveraging data is a combined engineering/architectural discipline; how data leveraging is key to accomplishing data strategy; knowing when your organization reaches appropriate maturity; and that these concepts are particularly applicable in application-centric, package-heavy environments.

CHAPTER 4

Focusing DM to Meet Common Organizational Challenges

4.1 CHAPTER OVERVIEW

All organizations perform DM activities – the relevant questions are:

1. How critical to organizational success are they?; and
2. How well prepared is the organization to address their DM challenges?

Leveraging data in support of strategy remains a common organizational challenge. Organizations are performing DM poorly. Perhaps more importantly, responsibility for addressing the gaps is at best ill-defined, and at worst, an unrecognized challenge. Objective measures of the "health" of DM practices worldwide presented below indicate that the typical organization is not able to leverage data in support of strategy.

4.2 UBIQUITOUS DM CHALLENGES: COMPLEXITY, DEGREE, AND SCOPE

DM as an industry has not been much studied.[1] There are few formal measures. Unlike software engineering, even relatively simplistic order of magnitude sizing calculations cannot be made reliably (McCabe 1976). When it is clear that an organization can benefit from effective and efficient (or what are called, 'advantageous' DM practices), the next evaluative step is to determine the DM challenge characteristics.

An organization's relative data challenge 'size' is a question of degree and complexity (Figure 4.1) within a defined scope. Organizations demonstrate that they believe that by increasing their DM proficiencies, their use of data to support strategy will improve. DM value can be readily concretized as increases in the number of data aggregators and organizations selling training on how to access, for example, Walmart's Retail Link® portal.[2]

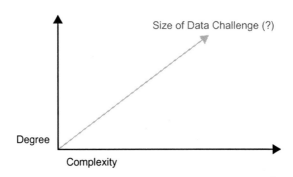

Figure 4.1 Data challenge 'size' is a function of degree and complexity within a defined scope.

[1] For example data topics comprise around under 7% of a major research keyword index – this is disproportionately low and constrains research opportunities (see http://www.acm.org/about/class/1998)

[2] Retail Link® is a registered trademark of WalMart Stores, Inc. – see also for example:http://datablueprint.comhttp://lexisnexis.com.   http://www.locationawhere.com/19/12/2009/companies/awhere-inc. http://www.acceleratedanalytics.com/blogcontent/making-the-most-of-retail-link-data.html. http://www.8thandwalton.com/courses (all accessed 1/17/2013)

Perhaps all the talk of the impending data deluge has them taking note (Economist 2010). DM was projected to be a $4 billion dollar annual market in 2012 (Bernstein and Haas 2008) and US President Obama highlighted DM as a "skill that businesses are looking for right now!" in his 2012 State of the Union message (Obama 2012).

4.2.1 Complexity

Organizational DM complexity can be assessed by subject area. Within subject areas, the data differs, different success levels are achieved, and different time-constraints are imposed on service deliveries but in aggregate it is easier to get a 360° picture within each area. Organizational DM challenges range widely but with no seeming correlation to organizational size. For example, it is possible and useful to develop expertise in the data of the Chemical Industry (CI) but it is generally not terribly complex to understand CI data. It is more complex to understand Wall Street data than CI data but CI data assumes that the human has mastered chemical engineering skills. While math is required and helpful, Wall Street data does not require mastery of skills required for chemical engineering. DM in the health care industry is particularly complex due to interactions among personally identifiable information, sunshine, intellectual property laws, etc.

4.2.2 Degree

Degree plays a role similar to complexity but is an organization/situation dependent characteristic. For example, a small, highly skill-focused organization (for example a medium-sized veterinary practice grossing $3 million annually) can be 'run' quite well using a single, integrated software package (the micro-ERP if you will). The more functionality existing in the micro-ERP, the less the DM challenge and the fewer the physical interfaces required.[3] The number of required interfaces is almost never zero. There are always specialized devices and systems requiring integration with the micro-ERP. These interfaces often require cumbersome (occasionally manual) data movement.

4.2.3 Scope

DM scope cannot, by definition, be encapsulated within one organizational area. The need for DM across the databases and systems exists for both the infrastructure and functional areas. DM scope relates to

---

[3]Recall that interface represents a sunk development cost and an ongoing maintenance expense.

specific activities, work products, and architectural components. DM work products should affect different activities, hence the governance need. For example, you may maintain common data for facilities, staff, organizations, and partner organizations. If these data are to be consistent across all these different application areas, there must be a DM activity maintaining common semantics and data values. Similarly complex interaction can exist between infrastructure and area applications.

Everyone faces data challenges varying in complexity, degree, and scope. Data broadly interacts with business, infrastructure, and IT architectures. The task is to identify data classes within subject areas, and architect/engineer the best data leverage strategy. Without a good understanding of the relative size of the data challenge (degree/complexity for a specific scope) facing your organization, investments in data cannot be justified. Initially, almost all organizations will require some help with their organizational data decisions.

There is a natural tendency to put off the strategic because its immediate accomplishment is not perceived to be critical to the day-to-day organization operations. If strategic DM is ignored too long, the IT systems and databases within the organization degrade, become disorganized, and expensive to maintain. These costs can be sharply contrasted with organizations that understand the strategic nature of metadata practices – developed and employed to accelerate IT development and maintenance/evolution. When data classes are properly managed, the ability to leverage the commonly defined data grows commensurately. Maturing too is interoperability, integration, and data conformity. Databases are fewer, interfaces are decreasing, consistency is increased, and reuse is improving.

4.3 OBJECTIVE ASSESSMENTS OF ORGANIZATIONAL DM

Measures indicate that organizational DM performance has been poor. These include: DM program success; data quality measurements; and subjective DM performance. Organization DM performance is not comprehensive across areas. DM has not been consistently applied. DM programs are seldom assessed for quality and effectiveness. To be both valid and comprehensive, DM program assessments must at least address:

- DM practices success assessment;
- DM visibility within the organization; and
- DM practices evolution.

4.3.1 DM Program Success: Self Assessment

The first author participated in a study of DM professionals (1981–2007) that revealed low DM practice maturity levels (Aiken, Gillenson et al. 2011). The survey measured the five DM practice areas according to the five CMM maturity levels (see below and also Figure 5.8 in Chapter 5).

CMM Levels (Y-axis)	Five DM Practice Areas
Initial	Data Program Coordination
Repeatable	Operational Data Integration
Defined	Data Stewardship
Managed	Data Development
Optimized	Data Support Operations.

Across these practice areas, the study showed average CMM level was between 2 and 3 – between REPEATABLE and DEFINED. Starkly, across these practices areas no aspect of DM was thoroughly DEFINED. Figure 4.2 indicates low averages, with the typical organization unable to recreate basic DM practices should they become confused. This

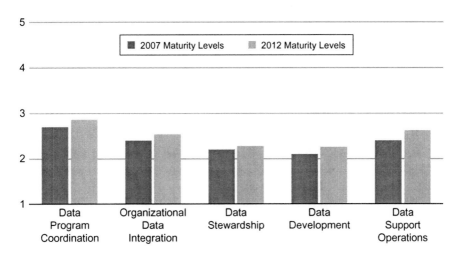

Figure 4.2 Industry-wide unrepeatable DM practices did not improve 2007–2012.

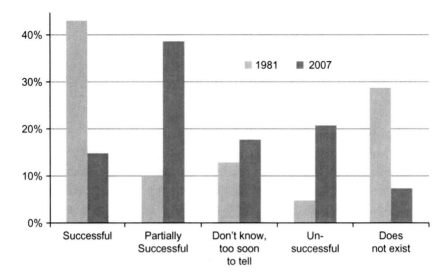

Figure 4.3 Does DM feel that it has been ... ?

effectively blocks any self-correction or improvement potential. Subsequent to the 2007 study, the general scores have not improved (in green) and only two organizations (out of 500+) have scored evidence of MANAGED DM practices.

Figure 4.3 illustrates one of the study's most striking findings — the marked decrease in the profession's collective assessment of its success — dropping from 43% in 1981 to 15% and the number labeled 'unsuccessful' increased from 5% to 21% in 2007 (Aiken, Gillenson et al. 2011).

This collective state-of-the-practice will remain true if the overall industry-wide DM performance remains uniformly low. If one competitor begins to out-perform the rest using better application of DM, the game will change quickly. Recall that industry adoption of RFID tags skyrocketed once retailers went RFID (Williams 2004).

4.3.2 DM Visibility Within the CIO Function
Over the past 25 years the DM group has moved down the reporting chain. As a priority, data has been pushed away from the CIO function.

1981	2007
74% reported to the CIO or 1-level down	43% reported to the CIO or 1- level down
26% reported at least 3-levels down	57% reported at least 3-levels down

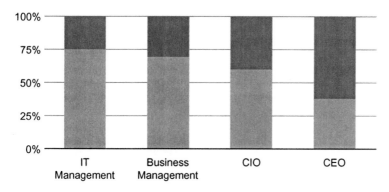

Figure 4.4 62% of CEOs are perceived as not understanding the strategic role of data.

These measures indicate widespread misunderstanding of data's strategic value. Too few, from CEOs on down, perceive the strategic value of data. Figure 4.4 indicates relative 'understanding' as rated by the 2007 survey of data managers. Fully one-quarter of IT managers and more than one-third of CIOs were seen as not understanding the strategic role data plays.

4.3.3 Measurable Data Quality and Responsibility for Data Quality

Much anecdotal evidence documents the costs of poor DM practices including:

- Excessive/unnecessary interfaces. Data quality is inversely proportional to the quantity of interface systems.
- Development delays due to low quality database designs; incomplete and unenforced value domains; inconsistent granularity; precision and data timeliness.
- Prohibitive migrations because of poor data quality, inconsistent semantics, and the data recollections.
- Excessively expensive data warehouse systems that either fail or consume resources well beyond original estimates due to data quality issues.
- Incorrect reporting of business transaction summaries due to ambiguous or outdated operational data.

We are unaware of any studies that show that data quality challenges are diminishing – all show the problem as large and growing

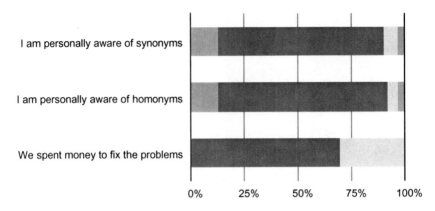

Figure 4.5 Red indicates widespread awareness of data quality issues. From (Aiken, Gillenson et al. 2011)

[see Figure 4.5, (Pipino, Lee et al. 2002), (Kahn, Strong et al. 2002), and (Redman 2008)]. Many measures of data quality costs have been reported — perhaps the most comprehensive case being Larry English's massive study accumulating more than 100 attributable, poor data quality stories amounting to over $1.2 trillion (English 2009)!

When researching data quality, two things become apparent. First, there is a fundamental misperception about whose problem data quality really is. When asked, survey after survey of non-IT knowledge workers indicate that data quality is the responsibility of IT, and IT believes that data quality is the responsibility of the business [see for example (Eckerson 2001)]. Second, data quality is not a primary concern for CIOs. Figure 4.6 illustrates that 49% believe IT responsible for data quality but this is not a universally held opinion as evidenced by the categories within the red circle.

> "Most think that this function is performed by the technology group — an already overwhelmed group of dedicated individuals who think that data quality is a function managed by the business. Clearly, the responsibility of this . . . has fallen between the cracks."
>
> **(Clarence W. Hempfield 2011)**

To summarize the objective data about organizational DM performance:

- Those closest to the DM practices rate their own levels of success low — widely unable to use DEFINED processes and very little evidence of excellence in practice.

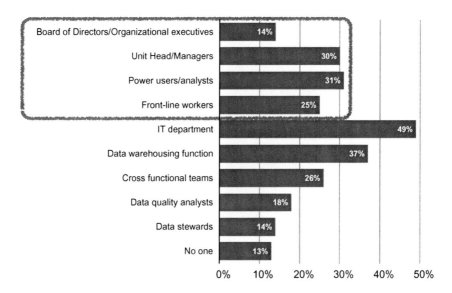

Figure 4.6 Who is responsible for data quality? Source: adapted from (Eckerson 2002)

- As the distance between DM and the CIO increased and the C-level understanding of data issues dropped.
- The data quality responsibility gap has not been addressed – both IT and the business hope the other is addressing the problem.

The ultimate responsibility for managing data as an asset is ill defined. As organizations rectify this situation with uniform DM practices, they will better cope with:

- Increasing scope and responsibilities.
- Improve the overall CMM levels.
- Improve C-level understanding of data asset leveraging.
- Unified CDO reporting.
- Codified skills and activities.[4]

4.4 WHY CIOs FAIL TO RECOGNIZE NEEDED DM IMPROVEMENTS

While the cause of this DM failure may seem puzzling at first, the reasons become clearer after examining the advice given to CIOs. Using

---

[4]At a recent professional gathering more than 300 titles were used by 1,200 attendees.

	2005	2006	2007	2008	2009	2010	2011
Grant Thornton-State CIO Survey		√	√	√	√	√	√
Ameritech ITAA Annual CIO survey	√	√	√	√	√	√	
CIO Magazine-State of the CIO			√	√	√	√	√
UK CIO Survey			√				
Gartner Annual Priorities	√	√	√	√	√	√	√
Informationweek Global CIO top 10 issues					√	√	√
Accenture CIO Survey			√				
KPMG & Harvey Nash		√	√	√	√	√	√
NASCIO Survey	√	√	√	√	√	√	√
Robert Half Technology		√	√	√	√	√	√

Figure 4.7 Source Surveys 2005–2011.

multiple annual CIO surveys, we created a concept map showing recent priorities. The data came from two sources – surveys of: 1) what CIOs reported as top priorities and 2) what industry experts advised CIOs. Figure 4.7 indicates the coverage of these 48 sources by year (for example – we were only able to locate the 2007 version of the UK CIO Survey results but all years of the Gartner Annual Priorities).

We assessed subjective DM performance data, comparing various priorities that CIOs and influencers of CIOs rated as their top five things to pay attention to – this year – each year for the seven years (2005–2011). The resulting ranks were inverted (i.e. the top ranked concern was given five points, the next ranked concern was given four points, etc.) and grouped by year. Because different years contained different numbers of concerns, we normalized each year's concerns – dividing by the total observations. Figure 4.8 summarizes this analysis.

Using a three-dimensional viewer, one could observe that IT/Information Security/Privacy has consistently been a top-five concern. The titles demonstrate that, as a CIO priority, little formal attention is paid to DM. There is an absence of DM topics beyond 'information sharing' and that only ranked in the top five during the year 2011. Many conversations with current and past CIOs confirm that DM is not on their radars.

Utilizing these sources, Figure 4.9 presents an array of CIO advocated focus areas. Notice that DM did not on make the list. This subjective data forces us a common observation: the CIO function's

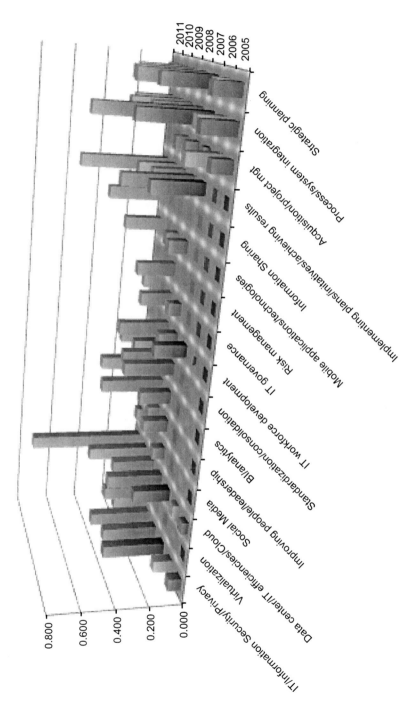

Figure 4.8 Evolution of top five CIO priorities 2005–2011.

Current Role Focus
- Aligning IT initiatives with business goals
- Improving IT operations/systems performance
- Cultivating the IT/business partnership
- Cost control/expense management
- Implementing new systems and architecture
- Leading change efforts
- Driving business innovation
- Redesigning business processes
- Identifying opportunities for competitive differentiation
- Developing and refining business strategy
- Negotiating with IT vendors
- Managing IT crises
- Developing market strategies and technologies
- Security management
- Studying trends/needs to identify opportunities

Figure 4.9 CIOs role focus areas.

distance (conceptually and organizationally) have resulted in losing touch with data-centric details/progress/concerns of data managers. Simply put, DM is not seen as a concern by CIO, or by those who advise them. This leads to one of three conclusions:

1. CIOs think DM is being adequately accomplished in their organizations; or
2. CIOs are unaware of the strategic nature of data; or
3. CIOs are not concerned about how DM is accomplished in their organizations.

We don't believe that conclusion 3 is true. The answer is a combination of 1 and 2. CIOs have been surprised when reminded of DM's foundational role in other organizational technology initiatives. Collectively, either they were not data-knowledgeable or they don't believe that improving their organizational DM performance is important to their success as CIOs.

4.5 WHY IT MIGHT BE DIFFICULT TO CHANGE THE STATUS QUO?

A natural tendency is to assume that the CIO function not only takes care of IT but also of data. From a title perspective, one could well argue that these are the logical groups to take on the CDO responsibilities. Indeed, many organizations are defining CDO roles that report to the CIO. There are two challenges with this arrangement: first, technology project implementation depends on data operating on a programmatic basis. Secondly, today's CIOs are most often really Chief of Information Technology or perhaps CTOs, in addition to being the Chiefs of Information. CIO concerns indicate that DM is either way down on the CIO's priority list or has fallen off altogether. In the prototypical organization, there would be no CIO, and the CDO would play a role in determining the information delivery agenda of the CTO. Solutions to this must come from universities, business information systems development practices, DM professionals and/or their professional associations, or a laser-like focus on DM by the CIO.

4.5.1 University DM Education

Studies from DAMA International indicate that DM professionals spent 10 years in other areas of IT before understanding data leveraging (Perez 2006). We need to find ways to shorten the process so that professionals realize data's important earlier in their careers. Recall that non-IT students learn little about systems, code, technology, etc. (but virtually all learn Microsoft's Excel). Organizations do not know that data is an asset and IT thinks that the answer to data management questions is technology. Curricula are in need of updating.

4.5.2 IT System Development Practices

New systems projects include the natural tendency to create new databases. Alternatively, interaction with an existing database is accomplished using interfaces. As 'new' development is preferred to 'maintenance' work, new systems are perceived as more 'exciting' and preferred. A prime reason existing databases are unable to serve multiple applications is that they have brittle designs – supporting tightly coupled programs/data and creating more data silos. It is natural to not want to slow systems development to prevent the creation of a new silo:

• The existing database that serves a specific function likely has to be redesigned. Who would pay for it?
• The existing system has to be modified to work with the revised database. Who would pay for that?

As a consequence, data silos grow constantly. So too do the data integration, interoperability, and non-redundancy challenges. Over time this degrades into a downward spiral increasingly reducing operational efficiencies. Organizational entropy is directly related to the quantity of data interfaces.

4.5.3 DM Professionals

Complicating the progress, most professionals are unaware of the definitional work done to date. The DAMA Data Management Body of Knowledge is an important first step in the right direction (DAMA-International 2009). For the first time: defined skill sets; methods; standard work product specifications; tool sets; certification;[5] and much more exists. These and related efforts need to become better known, in the same manner that project management concepts such as work breakdown structures and Gantt charts are now familiar to the larger knowledge worker community.

4.6 CHAPTER SUMMARY

While all organizations have data challenges of varying shapes and sizes, the DM status quo is simply this:

- For some very good reasons, CIOs have not see DM as a priority.
- Comprehensive, high quality DM must be developed and delivered outside of IT.
- Universities and training programs need to develop and implement DM courses and educational programs.
- DM professionals and their supporting professional organizations must provide more in-depth DM training, workshop and seminar materials.

[5]As of Q1 2013, more than 1,000 individuals worldwide have passed the CDMP examination and the phrase "CDMP Preferred" is seen more commonly on various job posting, including the one provided in Chapter 6.

CHAPTER 5

Creating the Right Conditions for CDO Success

5.1 CHAPTER OVERVIEW

Someone should be charged by the organization with the task of leveraging data assets in support of strategy. If we had to do it all over again, we are certain we would assign the CIO responsibility as the top data Chief. CIOs reading this book should consider:

Am I going to dedicate my career to the management of this increasingly critical organizational asset? That is, become more data-focused.

Or

Will I keep my current portfolio of IT concerns (technology focused) and help my organization obtain a dedicated resource to manage its data?

If the later alternative is chosen — welcome the evolution of your title towards CTO, IT Director, Director of IT, or something more accurately describing your challenging role — now resolved of the primary responsibility for organizational data.

While some temporary discomfort may come during the decision-making portion, only by dealing with the issue directly can an intelligent decision be made. The question is: is data receiving the 'care and feeding' required to leverage it? If data is important to the future of your organization you *must* establish a CDO function and then decide who should run it.

Regardless of your specific choice, where should the CDO be located, organizationally, and what should they be doing? The **where** section of this chapter describes the conditions required to achieve success and the **what** portion lists the top CDO priorities. This requires implementation of a rigorous regimen that touches all facets of the organization. In order to be successful CDO function requires three specific changes in most organizations — specifically the CDO should:

1. Focus on solely on data asset leveraging — these activities are outside of and more importantly both upstream and independent of any application system development lifecycle (SDLC) activities.
2. Report to the same organizational structure that the CFO and other 'top' asset management jobs report into; reporting outside of IT and the current CIO/CTO structure altogether;
3. Report directly to the business and concentrate on a crawl, walk, and run strategy — regularly and measurably improving the maturity of organizational DM practices.

5.2 WHERE SHOULD THEY REPORT?

The CDO is a business function and should not report to IT.

As organizations are embracing the CDO concept, 80% of them have this individual report to IT.[1] We strongly disagree with this concept. Appointing a CDO subordinate to the CIO (or any IT leader) forces data to be managed as part of the IT portfolio. The CDO *cannot* accomplish data leveraging while subject to the structured

---

[1] Our 2013 survey research also found that almost half CDOs had no budget, over half had no staff, and more than 70% thought they had insufficient organizational support.

deadlines of IT projects. Further, if they report through someone who is not data-knowledgeable, it will be impossible to improve the data decision-making process.

While transformation may require some organizational discomfort, this move will achieve improved organizational IT performance faster and cheaper than ERPs, Six Sigma, or any other silver bullet attempted to date.

5.2.1 The CDO Should Parallel the Reporting Structure of Other Asset Chiefs

The CDO should be the senior organizational official most expert in, and responsible for, organizational use of data-based organizational assets in support of strategy – the Data Chief. CDOs must implement a demanding regimen that touches all facets of the organization with a renewed emphasis on quality, decision-making, improving product/service, and a DM system that extends to organizational components.

There are two reasons why the CDO should report with the top organizational management team (see Figure 5.1). First, the historical low priority given to this function requires, at least for the next round, a corresponding bias towards data-centric development practices. Second, it is also clear that DM expertise is not widely available – organizations will need time to determine what works best for them and it will be while before generalized guidance is forthcoming. Actual implementation will require practiced coordination among IT, Operations, a specific domain (i.e. Marketing), and Data – with project specific domain rotation.

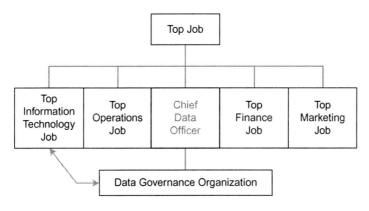

Figure 5.1 Positioning the CDO.

5.2.2 Arguments for not Reporting to IT

There are at least six arguments for *not* having the CDO subordinate to IT.

1. **IT does not feel the true impact of poor DM practices.**
   Data problems can and often do delay IT projects. This causes the organization to pay more for IT than it should. The impact to the organization is greater than IT. The organization is more likely to suffer publicly from data problems while the impact of IT-related data failures is less likely to become know to the outside.
2. **IT does not know organizational business rules that govern data and its use.**
   IT's focus on technical knowledge leaves little resources and few cycles to devote to understanding how data is used by the business for various decisions.
3. **IT does not own or control access to the subject matter expertise ultimately needed to implement data-centric development practices.**
   The technological focus keeps IT fully occupied with 'how' concerns. There is very little capacity for understanding business oriented, 'what' problems.
4. **Only the business can competently assign values on various data uses.**
   Defining what are 'good enough' DM practices cannot be done from an IT perspective.
5. **Reporting to IT has been expected because IT owned the method.**
   Because IT specializes in methods, IT was assumed to manage the data. Most non-IT knowledge workers have no idea that methods can be used to develop flexible, adaptable, and reusable data.
6. **CIOs are already slammed.**
   Anyone disagree?

5.2.3 Arguments for the CDO being Independent of IT

There are at least four arguments *for* CDO to be independent of IT.

1. **Appropriately apportions labor.**
   Because IT is already overloaded and has its hands full with the technology 'hows' focus of the organization's application systems, as well as all the other hardware, networks, and systems software it is appropriate that the CDO take ownership of defining the business 'what' focus.

2. **Reduces project-centric application system requirements.**
The traditional IT life cycle is highly focused on project-centric work products, implementations, and evolutions that foster and grow silos. In contrast, the CDO's efforts are organization-centric work products that are often project independent and that tend to eliminate IT silos. Again, these are essential, not accidental differences that result in fundamental impedance mismatches.
3. **Encourages business to learn appropriate IT-derived methods.**
Maintaining the requirements (the 'whats') in the business will reduce translations and encourage broadly based, data-centric, systems thinking. Business engineering is less rigorous than information systems engineering.
4. **Encourages organization-wide data and architectural component reuse.**
The longer-term focus of data is at odds with IT development cycle – DM is a program not a project. Nurtured data architectures grow in value and use over time.

On this point, we find growing agreement from the business as well as from the CIOs – they readily acknowledge they haven't the time or resources to focus on DM and they are happy for someone to assume these responsibilities.[2] They understand that asking IT to excel at the CDO's data mandate, in addition to all the other IT tasks, may be difficult. There are fundamental philosophical and operational mismatches between IT and DM. Organizational patience and discipline required to leverage data assets are at odds with the innovation-driven, technology focus prevalent in IT.

5.3 WHAT SHOULD THEY DO? PRIMARY CDO CHALLENGES

So assuming you are able to successfully argue for the business accepting the CDO role, what should this individual focus on? The answer is, in three parts:

1. Make DM independent from business information system development
2. Remain data focused
3. Improve your organization's DM maturity

[2]75% of our 2013 CDO survey respondents also favored reporting to the business.

5.3.1 CDO Scope

As part of the organization's senior leadership, the CDO is the head of organization-wide data governance – ensuring that the right things are done in the right way. The data scope of the CDO is not just business-centric 'real' data but also all the metadata across the entire organization. The CDO is responsible for improving the organization's data and data structures, culling the 80% data ROT suffered by most organizations (reducing data volume), and enriching the remainder (data quality). What remains, is the unique authoritative, and identifiable data and definitions desired by the organization – the master definitions – managed. Figure 5.2 shows how CDOs are marshaling a broad range of capabilities in support of data leveraging.

Figure 5.3 show all current DM functions except for two (Data Development and Database Operations Management) moving out of IT. Two DM functions (Metadata Management and Data Security Management) are explicitly shared with IT operations. This is a major shift – these functions are used to reporting to IT.

Figure 5.4 shows that most CDOs are establishing control over governance/architecture and some are incorporating BI and compliance functions.

Figure 5.5 and Figure 5.6 show how complex the job of CDO is perceived to be, tallying a variety of desired capabilities and required traits, respectively.

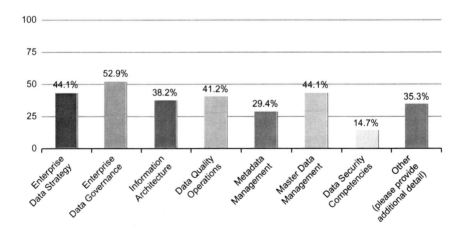

Figure 5.2 Tally of CDO capabilities (survey completed in Spring 2013).

Figure 5.3 Proposed division of DM Function between Business and IT. (adapted from http://dama.org/i4a/pages/index.cfm?pageid=3548)

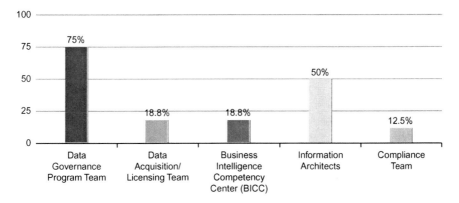

Figure 5.4 CDO reporting functions tallied (survey completed in Spring 2013).

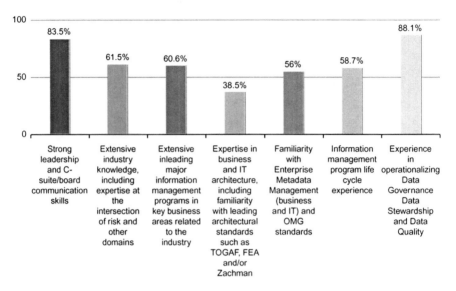

Figure 5.5 CDO Qualifications (survey completed in Spring 2013).

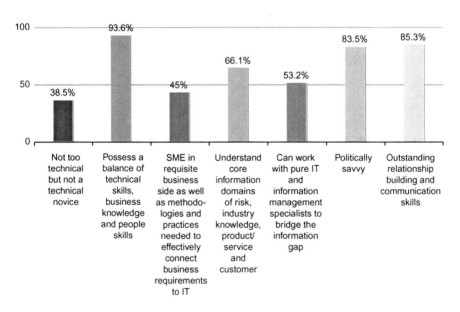

Figure 5.6 Required CDO Traits (survey completed in Spring 2013).

5.3.2 Make DM Independent from IT Development

A key difference exists between application systems and data architectures. Application systems either exist or they don't. The focus of
application systems development is to create something – where

nothing existed prior and to do it in a repeatable, standardized manner to minimize development costs. In contrast, data architectures are not created. Rather, they evolve. While all organizations have data architectures, the question is whether organizations are able to use their data architectures to support strategy. As such, the data architecture processes improve whatever data assets currently exist. Data architecture processes are more like maintenance, reengineering, and evolution processes while system development is focused on replacement.

The data architecture evolutionary approach is often foreign in strategy and execution when presented to typical IT professionals. It conflicts with the nature of application systems development. The results of a data architecture development effort provide a context for its subsequent IT application systems development projects. It can take years to evolve a data architecture from its current state to its desired state. This evolutionary effort can only be accomplished outside of the traditional application systems, project-centric development process.

Figure 5.7 illustrates an evolving data architecture that results from the step-wise refinement of different business information system development cycles. A number of SDLCs must properly occur in order for the DM activities to reach a critical mass past the tipping point and achieve the ability to usefully contribute in support of organizational strategy.

Over time, the number of requests for information architecture components increases as developers increase their understanding of data architecture methods and resources, and how to work these evolved understandings into their application system development plans. Similarly, as a data architectures increase in scope, the breadth and usefulness of its available data increases to system developers. Because of this data architecture discipline, each subsequent application system contributes enhanced data assets.

Evidence indicates that this back and forth interaction between IT application systems development and data architecture and evolution is simply not being performed in most organizations. Under the application system's development paradigm, data architectures are created entirely within application system's boundaries and are thus unusable by other parts of the organization. Data leveraging is prevented.

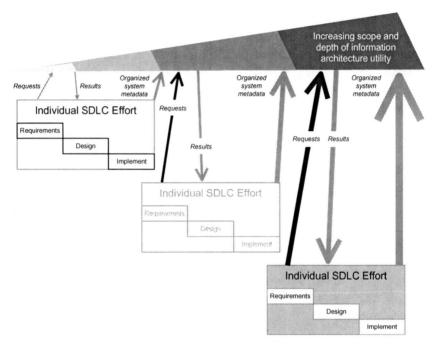

Figure 5.7 Individual SDLC efforts make increasing use from IA.

5.3.3 Remaining Data Focused – this is a Full Time Effort (FTE)

As part of a study, IT professions specializing in articulating system requirements were asked "What is the most difficult part of analysis?" The surprising answer that came back was a resounding "Not doing design!" That is, IT professionals focused on specifying "what" have a hard time not automatically following the 'what' with solution design. That wouldn't be such a challenge if time was *not* a factor. However requirements phases are time-boxed – any time spent doing design work directly robs time and attention from requirements. This is particularly damaging to organizational development efforts because it costs significantly more to identify and correct errors as an application system project progresses through the SDLC.

The CDO is a full-time job. As a senior leader within the organization, the CDO officer must maintain a sole focus on understanding, marshaling, and applying organizational data resources in support of strategy. The basic argument is that any time the CDO is paying attention to anything other than data support for strategy, they are diluting their own effectiveness.

5.3.4 Improve General DM Practice Maturity

DM has existed in some form since the 1950s and has been recognized as a discipline since the 1970s. DM is a young discipline when compared to the relatively mature accounting profession, which has existed for thousands of years. As Figure 5.8 shows, DM consists of five inter-related and coordinated practices. The figure supports the definition: "Organization-wide management of data is understanding the current and future data needs of an organization and making that data effective and efficient in supporting business activities" (Aiken, Allen et al. 2007).

The figure illustrates how strategy guides other DM practices. Two of these practices – Data Program Coordination and Organizational Data Integration – provide direction to the implementation practices – Data Development and Data Support Operations. The Data Stewardship practices straddle the line between Direction and Implementation. All practices exchange feedback designed to improve and fine-tune overall DM. Each practice is assessed according to the CMM five stages of maturity for process improvement. Process maturity assessment on the CMM scale yields both a baseline and direction, which, in turn, permits organizations to understand the nature of their organizational challenge [see (Aiken, Allen et al. 2007) for more detail] to achieve greater maturity. Increased maturity leads to increased data leveraging opportunities.

5.3.5 CDO Position Description

We have included a CDO position description that has allowed a number of our clients to recruit and hire satisfactorily qualified candidates.

TITLE: CHIEF DATA OFFICER

REPORTS TO: TOP JOB

POSITION SUMMARY:

This position has the overall responsibility for team-lead definition, engineering, and execution of organizational real- and meta-data architecture strategy including the planning, funding, training, development, integration, deployment, recovery, and evolution functions that are required to effectively and efficiently deliver data architecture

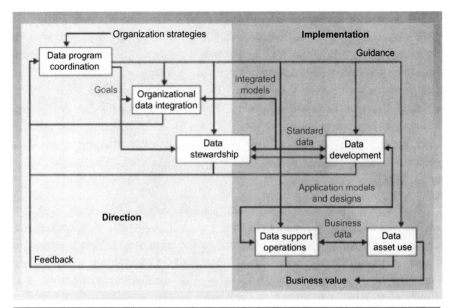

Practice Name	Description	Concerned with	Function Focus:
Data Program Coordination	Provide appropriate DM process and technological infrastructure	Data Program Data	
Organization Data Integration	Achieve organization data sharing of appropriate data	Data Development Data	Direction
Data Stewardship	*Achieve business-ebtity subject area data integration*	Data Stewardship Data	
Data Development	Achieve sharing of data within a business area		
Data Support Operations	Provide reliable access to data	Business Data	Implementation
Data Asset Use	Leverage data in business activities		

Figure 5.8 Organizational DM practice areas and their Inter-relationships (Parker 1999).

components that tangibly support the implementation of the organization's strategy.

RESPONSIBILITIES:

1. The position directs program-wide coordination of organizational data architecture activities to ensure maximal support for the

overriding concern − participating in the achievement of the business strategy. This includes ensuring that:

* Organizational data architecture activities are practiced in a coherent and coordinated manner − by defining, coordinating, resourcing, implementing, and monitoring organizational data architecture program strategies, policies, plans, etc. as a coherent set of activities beginning with the organizational data strategy and extending to all aspects of communication and execution including leveraging data assets to cut costs, accelerate growth, and foster innovation.
* Existing data is culled and specific subsets are selected to enhance their fitness for use.
* Data governance functions as the primary vehicle for implementing organizational data architectures. Data governance ensures that organizational data architectures remain efficient/effective and business driven. Data governance is recognized internally as the source of organizational expertise and best practices in governing the organization's information assets (such as use of standards). The data governance organization approves the data governance strategy, secures funding, and determines budgets/priorities for organizational information architecture.
* Organizational data architecture integrates itself into the existing architecture enhancement and application systems development processes in a manner that allows for synergistic growth with other architecture disciplines and that result in methods to continually advance organizational architectural capabilities.

2. Ensuring that the organization has an optimized, flexible/adaptable data distribution network (DDN) that is capable of delivering data in response to changing business dictates. DDN evolution is accomplished by identifying, modeling, coordinating, organizing, distributing, and architecting data shared across boundaries. The goal is to architect the improvement of organizational data exchange processes between programs, within organizational units, and between the organization and its business partners. The effectiveness of this DDN is the currency of organizational information architecture and this group must become recognized internally for its expert data delivery capabilities.

3. Ensuring that specific individuals are assigned the responsibility for the maintenance of specific data items as organizational assets, and that those individuals are provided the requisite KSAs to

accomplish these goals in conjunction with other data stewards in the organization. A strong governance/stewardship program ensures the development of organizational expertise and requires all participants to have up-to-date knowledge, skills, and abilities.

4. Continuously improving the effectiveness and efficiency of data delivery systems including database technologies, virtualization, services, etc. This involves specifying and designing appropriately architected data assets that are capable of supporting organizational needs using appropriate technologies and architectural patterns (cloud, SOA, MDM, warehousing, etc.). This must be accomplished with regard to and anticipation of future technology trends.

5. Governing the architecture and integrity of all real- and meta-data assets including: the initiation, operation, tuning, maintenance, backup/recovery, archiving and disposal of data assets in support of organizational activities. Responsible for ensuring that the data assets are, and will be available for required business purposes under various evaluated risks (business continuity/disaster recovery).

REQUIREMENTS:

Must be results oriented with superior leadership skills to inspire and motivate staff.

Demonstrated critical thinking skills, excellent communication, interpersonal relations and negotiation skills are essential as well as strong administration, organizational, analytical and problem solving skills.

Supervises and is responsible for overseeing work that is highly complex and varied in nature. Develops integrated solutions to achieve highly complex technical and business objectives. Must be a subject matter expert and have a strong understanding of present and future data utilization. Must have direct experience in data architecture, modeling, integration, design, quality engineering to implement various data strategy components. Must demonstrate success in planning, development and support of data infrastructure-based support for the company strategy.

Position requires a bachelor's degree in Computer Science, Information Technology or related field (advanced degree desired), ten to fifteen years of progressive responsibility including executive leadership ability. **CDMP preferred!**

5.4 THE PERHAPS TEMPORARY NATURE OF THE CDO

It should be noted that the need for certain Chief Officers has occasionally been temporary. The title Chief Electrification Officer isn't in as widespread use today, as it was during the when organizations were scrambling to learn how they could use electricity to support their business objectives. It is good and appropriate that these positions evolve in response to conditions and organizational needs. To be safe, we would suggest that for the first year the CDO focus 100% on organizational data issues.

Our 2013 research indicates that 53% of organizations recognize the need for a CDO but have not yet started the process of establishing the position. 5% indicate their CIO is covering these responsibilities and 8% indicate someone besides the CIO is accomplishing data asset leveraging. 7% were in the process of establishing or hiring their CDO. 1% believes that data plays a role small enough to not warrant a CDO.

For the other 99% we believe CDO should examine your data operating environments with an eye toward improvement.

5.5 CHAPTER SUMMARY

The CDO — where and what?

Where: the chief data officer must not exclusively report to IT — this content and subject matter knowledge exists outside out of IT. The CDO should report at level comparable to the chiefs of your other organizational resources.

What: Data-centric practices form the data advantage needed by the organization and can be boiled down to the top three items:

1. Make DM independent from IT system development
2. Remain data focused
3. Improve your organization's DM maturity

CHAPTER 6

Conclusions/Suggestions

To summarize:

- CIO function is already hugely demanding!
- Unique and/or context-specific DM challenges require development of specialized disciplines with unique knowledge, skills, and abilities!
- Educational institutions are not addressing the challenge!
- Some drastic changes are required!
- The CDO is the first step in the right direction

Reconsider and reevaluate these roles in your organization. Most will opt to start moving in the direction of the CDO and address the lack qualified personnel and/or organizational focus. Organizational strategy increasingly depends on your organizational data assets.

The need for a newly defined executive level role for data/information ownership is clear, and is distinct from the role of leading IT. CDO success depends on the factors described – including:

- Making data separate from technology.
- Maintaining a data focus – having the CDO begin as a full time position with the right tools/methods.
- Ensuring that the CDO's activities, processes, methodologies and work products are subject to continuous improvement according to some agreed upon roadmap.
- Ensuring that DM work products are stored and employed in a manner that supports development of increasing integration.
- Formally defining, implementing and following DM's key process areas.
- Ensuring that the CDO operates mainly from the business functional side of the organization so as to build the data leveraging practices.
- Understanding the five DM practices areas are necessary but insufficient prerequisites to organizational data leveraging applications (aka self actualizing data, or advanced data practices shown in the green portion of Figure 6.1).

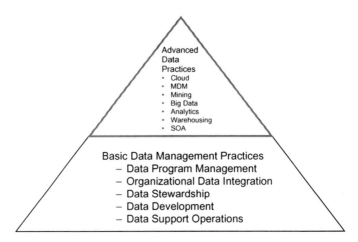

Figure 6.1 Like Maslow, it is difficult to start sprinting when the foundational skills of crawling and then walking are not mastered.

This last is the biggest lesson organizations have learned over the years. Successes at the top of Figure 6.1 take longer, cost more, and delivery less than successes built on top of foundational DM practices. The CDO (reborn as a business focus) can help organizations maintain a singular focus on: *leveraging data as strategy!*

The data advantage is best realized through tangible measure such as increased productivity/quality, and decreased cost/risk. Virtually all business information systems have large data overlaps. This produces the common dimension for most business information systems is the data they share. When business information systems are accomplished via data-centric approaches, there can be fewer components to implement and maintain. Further, business information system generators can be brought to bear thus making business information system development efforts almost a 'silver bullet' (i.e. 7–10 times) quicker.

REFERENCES

Aiken, P. H., et al. (1994). DoD legacy systems: Reverse engineering data requirements. *Communications of the ACM, 37*(5), 15.

Aiken, P. H., et al. (2007). Measuring data management pratice maturity: A community's self-assessment. *IEEE Computer, 40*(4), 8.

Aiken, P. H., et al. (2011). Data management and data administration: Assessing 25 years of practice. *Journal of Database Management, 22*(3), 20.

Appleton, D. (1986). Information Asset Management. *Datamation*. Newton, MA: Cahners Publishing Company 32, 6.

Bernstein, P. A., & Haas, L. M. (2008). Information integration in the enterprise. *Communications of the ACM, 51*(9), 7.

Brown, T. (2012). *Smart people use smart phones*, from <http://appitive.com/technology/2012/12/30/smart-people-use-smart-phones/>.

CapitalOne (2013). *History - How we got started*, from <http://www.capitalone.com/about/corporate-information/history/?Log=1&EventType=Link&ComponentType=T&LOB=MTS%3A%3ALCTMJBE8Z&PageName=Corporate+Information&PortletLocation=4%3B4-8-4-col%3B2-3-1&ComponentName=History%3B2&ContentElement=1%3BLearn+More&TargetLob=MTS%3A%3ALCTMJBE8Z&TargetPageName=History>.

CIO. (n.d.) Computer Desktop Encyclopedia. (1981-2013). From < http://encyclopedia2.thefree-dictionary.com/CIO >.

Clarence W. Hempfield, J. (2011). *Data quality? thats its problem not mine what business leaders should know about data quality.* Pittney Bowes Business Insights.

Congress, U. (2002). *The Sarbanes-Oxley act aka public company accounting reform and investor protection act.* (U. Congress). Washington DC. (US Congress. 107-204 116 stat. 745).

Curran, C. (2009). *CIO Background check: IT experience mandatory?* (2013), retrieved from <http://www.cio.com/article/504149/CIO_Background_Check_IT_Experience_Mandatory_>.

DAMA-International (2009). *The guide to the data management body of knowledge.* Technics Publications, LLC.

dictionary.com (2012). Leverage. *<dictionary.com>*.

Eckerson, W. (2001). *TDWI data quality and the bottom line*. TDWI. 36.

Eckerson, W. (2011). Creating an enterprise data strategy: Managing data as a corporate asset. *BeyeResearch*.

Eckerson, W. W. (2002). Data quality and the bottom line: Achieving business success through a committment to high quality data. *TDWI Report Series*.

Economist (2010). Data, data everywhere: a special report on managing information. *The Economist*.

Economist_Intelligence_Unit. (2013). *Fostering a data-driven culture*.

English, L. P. (2009). *Information quality applied: Best practices for improving business information, processes and systems*. Wiley.

Friedman, T. L. (2005). *The world is flat: A brief history of the twenty-first century*. Picador.

Giuffrida, P. (2011). *The data focused CIO.*

Hayes, F. (2002). *The Story So Far.* (2012), from <http://www.computerworld.com/s/article/70102/The_Story_So_Far>(15.04.2002).

Kahn, B. K., et al. (2002). Information quality benchmark. *Communications of the ACM, 45*(4), 8.

Lewis, M. (2011). *The big short: Inside the doomsday machine.* W. W. Norton & Company. Reprint edition.

Marks, J. (2011). *Average tenure for agency CIOs is hovering at two years, GAO says.* Retrieved from   <http://www.nextgov.com/cloud-computing/2011/10/average-tenure-for-agency-cios-is-hovering-at-two-years-gao-says/49956/>(24.11.2012).

McCabe, T. (1976). A complexity measure. *IEEE Trans. on Software Engineering, 2*(4), 12.

McCafferty, D. (2011). *CIO job description: Which skills really matter?* 2013, from <http://www.cioinsight.com/c/a/IT-Management/CIO-Job-Description-Which-Skills-Really-Matter-842565/>.

Obama, B. (2012). 2012 State of the Union Address.

Olavsrud, T. (2012). Five steps for how to better manage your data. CIO, *CIO Magazine.*

Parker, B. G. (1999). Enterprise data management process maturity. In S. Purba (Ed.), *Handbook of Data Management* (pp. 824—843). Auerbach Publications, CRC Press.

Perez, A. (2006). The elusive species of the information age: The data management professional (Results of the 2006 DAMA International Survey). Unpublished: 6.

Pipino, L. L., et al. (2002). Data quality assessment. *Communications of the ACM, 45*(4), 9.

Porter, M. (1980). *Competitive strategy: Techniques for analyzing industries and competitors.* New York, NY: Free Press.

Redman, T. C. (2008). *Data driven: Profiting from your most important business asset.* Harvard Business School Press.

Wailgum, T. (2009). *The world's most underpaid CIO runs IT at the world's largest retailer.* Retrieved from <http://www.cio.com/article/500755/The_World_s_Most_Underpaid_CIO_Runs_IT_at_the_World_s_Largest_Retailer>(25.11.2012).

WEBCPA, S. (2010). *CFO tenure appears to be lengthening,* from <http://www.accountingtoday.com/news/CFO-Tenure-Lengthening-53255-1.html>.

Wikipedia (2012). *Chief Information Officer.* Retrieved from <http://en.wikipedia.org/wiki/Chief_information_officer> (22.11.2012).

Williams, D. H. 2013, from <http://www.directionsmag.com/articles/the-strategic-implications-of-wal-marts-rfid-mandate/123667>(29.7.04).

CPSIA information can be obtained at www.ICGtesting.com
Printed in the USA
BVOW011730020613

322183BV00006B/178/P